ORIOLE PARK BRANCH
DATE DUE   11-02

DEC 11 2002			
JUL 1 7 2004			

DEMCO 38-296

BIRTHDAYS
AROUND THE WORLD

By

Mary D. Lankford

Illustrated by

Karen Dugan

HARPERCOLLINSPUBLISHERS

3

For Beth Bauer,
who gave Robert Lynn Lankford
the best gift — her hand in marriage on October 25, 1998.
—M.D.L.

For all the grandchildren of Karen and Norman LeBeau:
Mark and Sarah, Zachary and Adam, Matthew and Rebecca.
With love.
—K.D.

ACKNOWLEDGMENTS
Thanks to Cindy Chang for coming up with the idea for this book!

In writing this book, technology has allowed me to be in touch with people all over the world. Friends living or vacationing in other countries served as reporters — gathering information; verifying facts; communicating by e-mail, fax transmissions, telephone, and mail to provide essential information. As I followed various leads, I made new friends who were equally generous. This small thank-you is hardly enough acknowledgment of their friendship and assistance.

Pat Benner, Irving, Texas; Wilma Schleyer Bitel, Trophy Club, Texas, and Selangor, Malaysia; Jane Botham, Milwaukee, Wisconsin; Dr. John A. Crain, son, Jay, and wife, Elsa, DeKalb, Texas, and The Philippines; Subha Upan Dinayak, Selangor, Malaysia; Tamara Goonesena, Selangor, Malaysia; Mary Higbie, Irving, Texas; Beth Bauer Lankford, Dallas, Texas; John, Rosanna, and Ryan Lee, Tasmania; Liisa Levanan, Finnish Consulate, New York, New York; Marisa Miller, New York, New York; Johan Nylen, Sweden; Fiona Ong, Selangor, Malaysia; Esko Pajarinen, Raahe, Finland; Julie Judd Pankey, Dallas, Texas; Judy Phoon, Selangor, Malaysia; Elizabeth Risk, Christ Church, South Island, New Zealand; Artice Tate, Irving, Texas; Heli Vuoti, Oulu, Finland; Inge Woolley, Dallas, Texas; Gertjan Zwiers, The Netherlands; all the Australian students who sent information about birthdays.

Library of Congress Cataloging-in-Publication Data
Lankford, Mary D.
   Birthdays around the world / by Mary D. Lankford ; illustrated by Karen Dugan.
     p.   cm.
   Includes bibliographical references.
   Summary: Describes the way birthdays have been celebrated in the past and the customs used to mark these special occasions in such countries as Finland, Malaysia, Mexico, New Zealand and others.
    ISBN 0-688-15431-X (trade) — ISBN 0-688-15432-8 (library)
    1. Birthdays — Cross-cultural studies — Juvenile literature. [1. Birthdays.]
I. Dugan, Karen, ill. II. Title.
GT2430.L35 2002   99-49779
394.2 — dc21   CIP
                                                           AC

Typography by Elynn Cohen 1 2 3 4 5 6 7 8 9 10 ❖ First Edition

CONTENTS

BIRTHDAY SONG

(Anonymous)

In heaven shines a golden star.
An angel led me from afar,
From heaven high unto the earth
And brought me to my house of birth.

Oh, welcome, welcome, lovely day
With sunshine bright and flowers gay,
With painted birds that sing their song
And make me kind and good and strong.

AUTHOR'S NOTE

HEN I WAS A CHILD, we often celebrated birthdays with my mother's parents. My birthday is on December 7, and I was filled with anticipation on the sixty-mile trip to Grandmother and Granddad Bass's home in Chico, a small north Texas town. I knew the birthday cake would be served on my favorite blue dishes, made of what was called Depression glass, which my grandmother collected from boxes of oatmeal. In those years, as an incentive to buy, it was quite common to find a prize in various types of boxed food. It didn't matter to me that the blue plates were free. I thought they were beautiful. I always requested a three-layer chocolate cake with chocolate icing. The cake was topped with candles and white icing that spelled "Happy Birthday, Mary D."

We always played Pin the Tail on the Donkey and Musical Chairs. In another favorite game, one child, holding a clothespin beside his or her nose, leaned over and attempted to drop the clothespin into a bottle. Other children tried to make the person dropping the clothespin laugh.

As I planned birthday parties for my children, the world had changed. There were no special blue glass plates in oatmeal boxes. We used colorful paper plates with napkins that matched. Many of the games, though, remained the same.

I always learn many new and interesting facts when I write a book. This book about birthday customs and traditions is no different. Despite variations in cake, party, or language of the birthday greeting, one theme is true for all countries: The birth of a child is special. Good wishes, congratulations, and honoring a child or an adult on his or her birthday remain the same throughout the years. I hope you can always blow out all the candles on your cake with one breath and that the wishes made on those candles come true.

Mary D. Lankford

INTRODUCTION

MOST PEOPLE are unique in their appearance, personality, likes or dislikes, where they live, and what they do. But one thing that isn't unique about us is our birthdays. If you're a twin or one of a multiple birth, you already know one person — or more — who shares your birthday. Or you may have a friend who was born on your exact month, day, and year of birth. Even if you don't, every year, on your own special birthday, many, many other people are celebrating the same birthday all over the world.

Without calendars there never would have been any birthdays at all. Long ago people had no way to mark the passage of time. Eventually calendars were invented and the passage of time was divided into years, months, and days. Slowly the custom of celebrating one's birth began.

At first only very powerful people were honored with birthday celebrations. The Roman emperor Caesar Augustus held a birthday celebration each month! But then the common people began celebrating too. In those days just living to your next birthday might be cause for rejoicing. Or perhaps people wanted to take every opportunity to give their loved ones good wishes or gifts to keep evil spirits away. In some cultures a mock spanking is given to the birthday person. This custom probably began as a tribal rite to make the body pure. Once the spanking was over, the person was welcomed back to the group and offered congratulations, well wishes, and good luck.

Early Christians believed it was sinful to rejoice on a birthday. Church festivals were centered, not on birthdays, but on the death days of the saints. Saints are people who performed great services for Christianity. In some cultures, when a child is born, at least one of his or her given names is a saint's name. A child may be named after a saint whose feast day, or day of celebration, coincides with the day on which the child was born. The child then honors, or celebrates, his birthday on the Saint's Day, or Name Day.

The ancient Greeks traditionally honored the birthday of Artemis, goddess of the moon, marriage, and childbirth, by placing a moon-shaped cake topped with candles on an altar in her temple.

Years later, Germanic people celebrated birthdays with a cake and candles, but the candles were not put on the cake. Instead these first birthday candles were set on the plate or the table, surrounding the cake in a circle of light. The candles burned throughout the day, until the evening meal.

Blowing out the candles and making a wish is another way of wishing ourselves good luck.

Throughout the world we celebrate the birthdays of people we honor. The birth of Jesus Christ is celebrated on December 25. This Christmas celebration forms a common bond among people of the Christian faith. April 8, the day of the birth of Shaka, a name for Buddha, is celebrated by millions of Buddhists in Sri Lanka, Tibet, Nepal, Burma, Vietnam, Korea, China, Japan, and elsewhere worldwide. Some countries have national holidays to honor historical leaders. In the United States we honor the birthday of Martin Luther King, Jr., on the third Monday in January. Abraham Lincoln's and George Washington's birthdays are celebrated the third Monday in February.

Certain birthdays are considered special in some countries. In Japan, children's third, fifth, and seventh birthdays are celebrated on November 15, the holiday *Shichi-go-san*. Many cultures have a birthday that signifies the move from childhood to adulthood. For example, a Latina girl celebrates her fifteenth birthday with a party called a *quinceañera*.

Whether you celebrate at home or school, wear funny hats, eat cake and ice cream, play games, or receive gifts, you are taking part in a tradition that began hundreds of years ago. Birthday celebrations continue throughout the world so that we can tell people we are happy they were born.

FINLAND

One third of Finland lies within the Arctic Circle. Smaller than the state of Montana, Finland has a landscape enhanced by sixty thousand lakes and sixty-five hundred islands. Forests cover almost three-fourths of the low, flat lands and rolling hills. During the long winter nights, the sky is brightened by the beautiful colors of the aurora borealis, or northern lights. Daylight in summer may last nineteen hours, and the sun, when it does set, barely dips below the horizon.

A FINNISH CHILD'S birthday celebration is a very important event to the entire family. Most birthday parties take place on a Saturday or Sunday so that everyone can gather at the home of the birthday boy or girl. Friends greet the birthday "hero" with *Onneksi Olkoon!* which means "To your happiness!" The Finnish tradition is to open gifts as soon as they are received.

The "Happy Birthday to You" song, written about one hundred years ago by Americans Mildred J. and Patty Hill, is sung in Finland and all around the world. Unlike children in the United States, who sing at the table when the birthday cake is being served, Finnish children sing it at the door when they arrive at the party.

A traditional Finnish birthday cake is cut to make three layers. The filling is a mixture of strawberries, bananas, and whipped cream. Candles, one for each year being celebrated, are almost hidden by toppings of whipped cream, candies, kiwi, or strawberries. The cake is served as dessert, after a lunch of party foods such as sausages and salads. A summer birthday party might include a cooling drink of *sima,* or Finnish lemonade.

A popular Finnish birthday game is called *Onginta,* which means Angling or Fishing. Taking turns, each child stands in front of a piece of cloth held up by adults. A rod attached to a line with a hook on the end is lowered over and behind the cloth to fish for a prize. An adult standing behind the cloth attaches a small basket on the hook. The child reels it in and finds a small prize inside.

MALAYSIA

Eleven of the thirteen states that make up the Land of Eternal Summer, or Malaysia, are on the Malay Peninsula. The other two are four hundred miles away on the island of Borneo.

There is a link between Malaysia and the eraser on your pencil. In the 1800s rubber plant seeds were smuggled out of Brazil and brought to Malaysia. Its hot climate, dense rain forests, and abundant rainfall were perfect for rubber trees. Pencil erasers are just one of the rubber tree's many products.

ETHNICALLY, RELIGIOUSLY, and culturally diverse, Malaysians may be of Chinese, Indonesian, European, Indian, or Malaysian descent. Many Malaysians follow the religion of Islam. Islamic men practice an important religious duty by offering five prayers daily. The greeting that is whispered to newborn Muslim babies by their fathers or grandfathers is the Call to Prayer. Thus, the first words a Muslim hears will also be the last at his or her burial.

Honoring an old custom, Malaysian women of Asian descent sometimes remain inside the home for forty-four days following their baby's birth. No doors or windows can be opened because, according to tradition, wind is bad for both mother and baby. The full moon after the forty-fourth day marks the first time they can go outdoors. For this special day the mother prepares noodle soup. The noodles represent long life, since they are long and straight. The most important celebrations are the baby's first full moon and first birthday.

The birthday greeting in the Malay language is *Selamat hari jadi*. Malaysian Chinese greet the birthday child saying, *Sen yat*. In the Chinese tradition an extra birthday is celebrated on the seventh day of the new year. On this "birthday for everyone," people are urged to eat uncooked lettuce and raw fish, especially carp. The Chinese word for "raw," 生, also means "life" or "to grow"; therefore, eating fresh vegetables and fresh fish is symbolic of enjoying a long and prosperous life.

On the actual individual birthday, family and friends may give red paper packets, or envelopes, containing money. Given in even amounts, money is considered lucky. It is bad manners to open red packets in the presence of the giver or other guests.

A birthday ribbon cake, made with alternating layers of cake and colored butter, is served. The traditional American birthday tune is sung in English. A traditional birthday game is Pass the Box. Wrapped in bright colors, the box is passed from child to child. When an adult says, "Stop!" the person holding the box must sing a song.

MEXICO

Mexico City is not only the capital of Mexico but also the largest city on the American continents. Mexico's border to the east is the Gulf of Mexico and, on the west, the Pacific Ocean. Miles of volcanic sand beaches provide flat surfaces for playing the popular *fútbol,* or soccer.

Because most people in Mexico are Catholic, young people may celebrate two birthdays each year—one on their day of birth and the other on the day of the saint whose name they are given. Of course, this happens only if the days are not the same.

ON THE DAY of the birthday party, the house may be decorated with beautiful paper flowers. The greeting *Feliz cumpleaños,* or "Happy birthday," is repeated many times. Mexican children celebrate with a birthday cake and candles, but they get *three* wishes if they blow out the candles with one breath! Friends, after giving a gift, may attempt to give *chetes,* or spanks. Breaking the piñata, a gift-filled colorful papier-mâché container shaped like an animal, clown, or popular character, is usually the highlight of the party.

After cake is served, the game of Coyote and Sheep may be played with up to twelve players. One person, the Shepherd, takes his place at the head of the line. Sheep form a line behind the Shepherd, placing their hands on the waist of the player in front. The other player is the Coyote. The game begins when the Coyote approaches and the Shepherd asks, "What does the Coyote want?"

The Coyote answers, "I want fat meat!"

The Shepherd calls, "Then go to the end of the line, where the fattest Sheep are."

The Coyote runs to the end of the line, trying to tag the last Sheep. The Shepherd defends the flock by extending his arms and running in all directions, attempting to prevent the Coyote from touching the last Sheep. The line of Sheep helps by weaving back and forth. The Sheep and Shepherd must not break their line. If they do, the Shepherd becomes the next Coyote and the next man in line becomes the Shepherd. The same thing is true when the Coyote tags the last player.

THE NETHERLANDS

The Netherlands, whose name means "low land," is a coastal country in Western Europe. Much of its land was once under the North Sea. Embankments, or dikes, are used to hold back the ocean. Long ago water was pumped from the land using windmills, but today diesel and electric pumps do the work. Through these efforts many acres of land have been added to the country.

CELEBRATIONS AT HOME in the Netherlands begin with family members decorating a birthday chair at the dining table. Both chair and walls might be decorated with garlands, called *slingers*. For a summertime birthday vases throughout the house are filled with blooms. The birthday child usually chooses food for the evening meal and stays up later than usual.

Traditional treats include very rich, elaborate pastries. Each party guest may get a different pastry, called *gebakjes*. A birthday cake, or *verjaardagh-taart*, is served without candles. For a very large or special birthday, an ice cream cake might be served with lemonade to drink.

A custom unique to the Netherlands is practiced when a man celebrates his fiftieth birthday. This is called reaching Abraham. This custom is based on a quotation from the Bible, John 8:57: "Then said the Jews unto him, Thou art not yet fifty years old, and hast thou seen Abraham?" Abraham figures—flat cookies about twelve inches long and decorated with edible beads—are purchased at bakeries and given to men on their fiftieth birthdays.

One of the games played at the party may be *Koekhappen*. Children are blindfolded and attempt to eat soft cookies hanging from a string.

Zakdoekje Leggen, or Drop the Handkerchief, is another traditional birthday game not only in the Netherlands but also in many other countries. Children sit in a circle about two feet apart. The child who is chosen to be *It* walks or runs around outside the circle holding a handkerchief. *It* can run one way or turn and run in the other direction. If someone is not paying attention, *It* drops the handkerchief to the floor behind him or her. That person quickly picks up the handkerchief, chasing after *It*, trying to touch him before he runs around the circle to the empty place. If he is caught, he must be *It* again. If he is not caught, the new person becomes *It* and begins circling to drop the handkerchief behind another person.

NEW ZEALAND

Thousands of years ago this country's first people, the Maori, called the land Aotearoa, or Land of the Long White Cloud. Dutch geographers changed the country's name to Nieuw Zeeland, after the Dutch province of Zeeland. Today the two-island country is known as New Zealand. Located in the Pacific Ocean, both islands are in a major earthquake zone. A visitor to New Zealand will find a remarkable variety of plants. Almost fifteen hundred species there are found nowhere else in the world. New Zealand has no snakes and only a few kinds of insects.

ALTHOUGH BOTH ENGLISH and Maori are official languages, birthday greetings are usually given in English. Maori is reserved for ceremonies or other special occasions. The morning begins with a gift from the family. The birthday will be announced on the radio if family or friends have sent in the name and birth date.

At school, especially in kindergarten and the early grades, each birthday child receives special mention or is given a birthday hat or badge. This is worn through the day and at home. Most birthday parties are still held at home, however. Favorite foods chosen by the honoree might include crisps, or chips, ice cream, and bread and butter topped with *hundreds and thousands,* or sprinkles, and, of course, a decorated cake.

A favorite birthday game is Share the Chocolate.

Guests are divided into two teams and form two lines. A chocolate cake, together with a hat, gloves, knife, and forks, is placed on a table a little distance from each team. The first player in each team runs to her team's chocolate cake, puts on the hat and gloves, cuts off a piece of chocolate, eats it, takes off the hat and gloves, and runs to the end of the line. The second team member repeats. The team finishing its cake first is the winner.

Another favorite game is Pass the Parcel. Guests sit in a ring, and a parcel wrapped with many layers of paper is passed from hand to hand as music is played. The guest holding the parcel when the music stops takes off one layer of paper and finds a small gift under that wrapping. Play continues until the last trinket is revealed when the final wrapping is removed.

THE PHILIPPINES

Invasions and attacks by Spain, Japan, Portugal, England, the Netherlands, and China and occupation by the United States have contributed to the fact that about eighty languages and dialects are spoken in the Philippine Islands. The principal languages are Pilipino, based on Tagalog, the language of many people native to the islands, and English.

IN TAGALOG birthday guests say, *Maligayang kaarawan,* or "Happy birthday." The reply when a gift is received is *Salamat,* or "Thank you."

Party food may differ from one region to another. A typical family birthday gathering could include a fruit salad made from pineapple, cherries, and the tropical yellow jackfruit. Jaz, a Philippine cola drink without bubbles, is served. As in many Asian countries, *pansit,* a dish with spaghettilike noodles, is prepared to symbolize long life for the birthday person.

Another part of the meal could be *adobo,* a dish made from chicken or pork and vegetables cooked with pineapple, vinegar, pepper, garlic, and salt. The menu might include a *lechon,* or roasted pig—head and all! These are popular dishes at fiestas and celebrations. If there is a cake, it is long, flat, and simply decorated with a birthday message.

The birthday piñata of the Philippines, a plain, undecorated clay pot, is part of the Spanish heritage. Children are blindfolded, spun around, then given a long piece of bamboo to break the piñata that is filled with candy as well as pesos and centavos, small-denomination coins.

A birthday party game is *Pusa at Aso,* or Cat and Dog. Players are the Cats and sit in a circle. One person, chosen to play the Dog, must remain seated in the middle of the circle. Near the Dog is a pile of shoes, sticks, stones, or objects representing a pile of bones. While the Dog guards his bones, the Cats attempt to steal them without being tagged. The Dog can tag the Cats only by touching them with his hands or feet. If the Dog tags a Cat, they exchange places. If the Cats get all the bones without being tagged, a new game begins with the same person playing the Dog.

SWEDEN

The Swedish people pride themselves on their leadership and independence. Sweden was the first European country to have a parliament in which all people were represented, not just those with wealth. Early in their history, Sweden gained independence from Denmark, and in the 1520s established Lutheranism as the state religion.

Each year, Sweden awards Nobel prizes to leaders from around the world for achievements in science, literature, and the promotion of peace. The prizes are named after Swedish chemist Alfred Nobel, who bequeathed $9 million for these awards.

SWEDISH CHILDREN WAKE on their birthdays hearing family members singing this song:

He should live a hundred years,
He should live a hundred years,
Yes, I wish that he shall live to know a hundred years.

Family members not only sing but also bring hot chocolate for the birthday child to drink before he gets out of bed. *Födelsedag,* or "Happy birthday," is the greeting of the day. A special gift is given from the entire family. This gift, such as jewelry, a pen and pencil set, or a watch, is usually something that can be used and treasured for a lifetime.

If a party for the entire class takes place at school, parents usually provide cake or ice cream.

The formal greeting, *Grattis pa födelsedagen,* or "Congratulations on your birthday," is used to greet the birthday child.

Instead of a birthday spanking, Swedish children give birthday "honors." Two people, one on either side of the birthday person, hold one of his arms and legs. He then swings back and forth, just above the floor, like a basket, while everyone shouts, *Ett fyrfacdigit leve,* or "Four times we honor you." Two swings are completed for each "honor" and one swing for each birthday being celebrated. Each year, on the first Sunday in March, many Swedish men celebrate their fiftieth birthdays by entering the *Vasalopp.* This is the biggest cross-country ski race in the world.

BIRTHDAY SUPERSTITIONS

IN PRIMITIVE TIMES in coastal regions it was the responsibility of the father to take a newborn baby to the sea and make a sign of the cross in salt water on the baby's left shoulder. This protected the newborn from evil.

Some families still carry the baby up a set of stairs, then down. This is based on an old superstition that only then will a child go up in the world before it goes down, or grows old.

Among people who live in coastal fishing regions, some believe a child cannot be born until the tide comes in. If a baby is born at ebb tide, it is considered a bad sign.

From Yorkshire, England, comes the belief that a child born at midnight is given a special power to see ghosts.

So that the child will have good luck, some say that after it is born it should first be held by a young unmarried girl.

Many still regard Sunday as the best day on which to be born and Friday as the worst. One superstition holds that children born on the first day of the month will have good fortune all through their lives. Perhaps this is because the number one is considered lucky. Some people believe that New Year's Day and Christmas are the best days to be born and that a child born on Christmas Day is twice blessed.

In Germany, there are those who look up at the clouds the exact minute a baby is born. If the clouds are shaped like sheep or lambs, the baby will have good fortune during its life.

The fifth day of the fifth month is considered an unlucky birthday.

A rhyme from Maine and Massachusetts concerns which is born first, a boy or a girl.

First a daughter, then a son,
The world is well begun.
First a son, then a daughter,
Trouble follows after.

A birthmark is believed by some people to be a good luck charm. Friends might even toss black pepper on an expectant mother, thinking that her child would then be born with birthmarks. Another belief is that more moles on the left side than the right may mean the child will be unlucky. An old English rhyme says,

A mole on your arm
Can do you no harm.
A mole on your lip
You're witty and flip.
A mole on your neck
Brings money by the peck.
A mole on your back
Brings money by the sack.
A mole on your ear
Brings money year by year.

The custom of decorating a birthday cake with candles may have originated in the ancient belief that a lit candle symbolized life. Such beliefs, cultural traditions, and sometimes a lack of understanding about natural events form the basis of wishing and superstitions. Many ancient customs are incorporated into our own celebrations.

Some people believe children will have bad luck if they are *not* spanked on their birthday. They should receive one spank for each year of age, and then one spank to grow on, one spank to live on, one spank to eat on, one spank to be happy on, and one spank to get married on.

Another belief is that a child who cries on his or her birthday will cry every day of the following year.

It has been said that the seventh child of a seventh child will be brilliant and become famous.

There is another old superstition that it is unlucky to be married on one's birthday.

In Russia, when a child is born, many parents plant a tree, thinking that the youngster's success in life will mirror the growth of the tree. In Switzerland tree planting also symbolizes good luck. A pear tree is planted for the birth of a girl and an apple tree for the birth of a boy.

The birth of a child is always a miraculous event. Years ago, when there was very little knowledge of medicine and good health practices, keeping a baby alive was difficult. Parents were eager to try anything—superstitions, wishes, and belief in magic—that might ensure good health for the baby. The long christening robes still used today may have originated in an effort to disguise the baby as an adult to fool evil spirits. Even today, we continue the tradition of making a wish and blowing out birthday candles to make sure that wish comes true.

WHAT MONTH IS YOUR BIRTHDAY?

DID YOU KNOW that certain gems, flowers, and even character traits have become associated with being born in each of the months of the year? The best thing about these customs is that they are fun and interesting and can be used for birthday themes and gifts. There are many variations, but here is a typical list.

MONTH	GEM OR STONE	FLOWER	CHARACTER TRAIT
January	Garnet	Carnation	Constancy
February	Amethyst	Violet	Sincerity
March	Aquamarine	Jonquil	Courage
April	Diamond	Daisy	Innocence
May	Emerald	Lily of the valley	Success in love
June	Pearl	Rose	Health and longevity
July	Ruby	Larkspur	Contentment
August	Carnelian	Gladiolus	Married happiness or friendship
September	Sapphire	Aster	Clear thinking
October	Opal	Calendula	Hope
November	Topaz	Chrysanthemum	Fidelity
December	Turquoise	Narcissus	Prosperity

AROUND THE WORLD BIRTHDAY PARTY

PART OF THE FUN in celebrating your birthday is helping to plan a party. Talk with the adults in your home to decide how many people can be invited, how much money can be spent, and where you can have the party. Consider which friends and family members you want to invite. A party with six to eight people is a good number.

Next, decide on a theme, or idea, for your party. The theme can be used for invitations, table decorations, and games. You can use this book as a source of ideas for your theme. You have read about birthday customs in seven countries. All seven have one thing in common: They are touched by an ocean. If you choose an Around the World Ocean Birthday theme for your party, use the following ideas.

Invitations: You will need construction paper, scissors, glue, and crayons. On construction paper, draw a fish shape for a pattern. Trace this shape on two pieces of paper for each invitation, and cut out the fish. Decorate them with scales, fins, eyes, and mouth. Put a small line of glue on all edges of the undecorated side, except the mouth opening. Place the two cutout fish together, decorated sides out. Allow the glue to dry completely. In the meantime cut out small fish to go inside the large fish. Each smaller fish will have the invitation information on it. Include the name of the party, your name, address, and telephone number, the date, and the beginning and ending times. After the glue has dried, open the large fish's mouth and put four or five crumpled tissues inside. Complete the invitation by placing the small fish inside the mouth of the larger fish. If you plan to mail your invitations, eliminate the crumpled tissues and make sure the invitations fit in standard-size envelopes.

Costumes: These are inexpensive and easy to make. Costumes represent countries touched by an ocean. You will need large brown paper grocery bags, glue, scissors, and crayons. Open the bag, and, with the help of an adult, cut a slit lengthwise in the middle of the bottom of the sack, almost to the sides. At each end of the long slit make an additional short slit. The result should look like this.

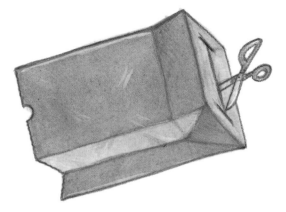

The bag will be pulled over the head, so that the slit on the bottom of the bag becomes the top of the costume around the neck.

Use scissors to cut a hole for an arm on each side of the bag as shown below.

left side

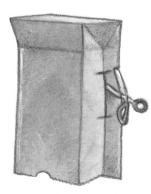

right side

Now comes the fun part. On one side of the bag draw either a sea animal or a flag from one of the countries touched by the ocean. If the bag has printing on it, glue on paper to cover it. This paper will be great for your drawing. As guests arrive, give them each a costume and a small plastic sand pail with their name on the side, which they will get to keep. The sand pail will be used for the first game that follows.

Select a number of prizes to be given to the winners of the following games.

Worm or Fish Toss Game: Give children gummy candy shaped like fish, worms, or dolphins. Make a line on the floor with a piece of masking tape or string. Players stand behind this line and try to toss their candy into their sand pail. Do not place the sand pails so far away from the line that they are impossible to hit. The child who gets the most candy into her basket gets a prize, and everyone gets to keep the candy.

Sea Cucumber Game: Use a large cucumber. Everyone sits in a circle and passes the cucumber around. When a whistle blows, the person holding the cucumber is out of the game. The last person remaining is the winner.

Fish Pong Game (played out of doors): Use a permanent marker to draw a fish design on each of ten Ping-Pong balls. Fill a small plastic swimming pool with water. Place the balls in the water. As players take turns, they use both hands to scoop up as many Fish Pongs as possible without stepping in the pool. The balls are counted, the score is recorded, and all the balls are returned to the water. Then the next person takes a turn. Each person gets three tries. The player with the highest overall score wins.

Table Decorations: Cover a blue or green tablecloth with a fishnet, seashells, or Goldfish crackers.

Starfish Sea Slurps: For ocean food, pour colored gelatin powder into a shallow pan. With an adult's help follow the directions on the package to dissolve the powder in boiling water. After the gelatin has set in the refrigerator, use a star-shaped cookie cutter to cut Starfish Sea Slurps.

Sea Snakes: Cut a hot dog lengthwise into six thin strips. As the strips cook in a pot of boiling water, they form twisting snakelike shapes.

Hotdog Octopus: Place a hot dog on a cutting board. Begin cutting one inch from one end and make a lengthwise cut, all the way through, all the way to the other end. Turn the hot dog and make as many lengthwise cuts as you can. Place in a pot of boiling water until it looks like an octopus.

Birthday Cake: Decorate the cake plate with crushed vanilla cookies to look like sand. Use white icing for the cake and squirt blue icing from a tube to form wave patterns on the sides of the cake. Decorate the top with candles inserted through Starfish Sea Slurps.

Prizes: As a reward for winning a game or for party favors, choose something connected to the ocean. Inexpensive seashell necklaces, flags of countries touched by the ocean, toy boats, aquarium objects such as treasure chests and mermaids are good choices.

GROWN-UPS—A BIRTHDAY BOOK CLUB

A BIRTHDAY BOOK CLUB makes it possible for students, parents, and staff to celebrate their birthdays by donating books to the school library. When I worked with school librarians in Irving, Texas, the clubs were organized in the following way. A parent-teacher organization provided funds to start the club and continued to support it. With these funds a librarian purchased books and placed them on a special shelf. A student celebrating his or her birthday could purchase a book at a price most students could afford. A bookplate noting the student's name and birth date was placed inside the purchased book, and the student received a certificate stating that he or she donated a book to the library.

If you feel that not all students may be able to purchase a book, try this idea from a librarian in Florida: Her school's parent-teacher organization provides money to purchase twelve birthday books each year. Every month a Birthday Book Party is held for students born in that month. Students with birthdays in June, July, and August celebrate at the end or the beginning of the school year. Each book carries a bookplate with the names of all the students born that month.

Or birthday celebrations might be held four times a year for students who have donated books. Another idea is to invite students to eat sack lunches in the library after donating a book. The library celebration concludes with cake and ice cream.

Consider the example of one school that photographed each student with his or her book and displayed the photograph on a bulletin board before it was glued inside the donated volume. A group photograph of an entire classroom is taken if the class donates a book as a holiday gift to the library.

In some schools students have donated books in honor of the birthdays of their dogs and cats!

Students as a class can donate money to purchase a book to honor the principal's birthday or those of teachers of special subjects such as music, art, and physical education. What better way to honor that person's birthday than by donating a book to the library?

It gives students great satisfaction to know that while their birthday may last only one day, the book they have donated will remain in their school long after they have graduated.

BIBLIOGRAPHY

Arnold, Caroline. *Everybody Has a Birthday*. Danbury, Conn.: Franklin Watts, 1987.

Ashley, Leonard. *The Wonderful World of Superstition, Prophecy & Luck*. New York: Dembner Books, 1984.

Barry, Sheila Anne. *Super-Colossal Book of Puzzles, Tricks & Games*. New York: Sterling, 1978.

Bel Geddes, Joan. *Childhood and Children: A Compendium of Customs, Superstitions, Theories, Profiles and Facts*. Phoenix, Ariz.: Oryx Press, 1997.

Cook, Debbie, and David Cook. *Malaysia, Land of Eternal Summer*. Kuala Lumpur: Wilmette Publications, 1995.

Culturgrams, The Nations Around Us, vols. 1, 2. Provo, Utah: Brigham Young University, 1997.

Feldman, Eve B. *Birthdays! Celebrating Life Around the World*. Mahwah, N.J.: Bridgewater Books, 1996.

Heaps, Willard A. *Superstition!* Nashville, Tenn.: Thomas Nelson, 1972.

The Holy Bible, King James Version. Cleveland, Ohio: The World Publishing Company.

Ingpen, Robert, and Philip Wilkinson. *A Celebration of Customs & Rituals of the World*. New York: Facts on File, 1996.

Jones, Alison, ed. *Larousse Dictionary of World Folklore*. New York: Larousse, 1996.

Jones, Betty M. *A Child's Seasonal Treasury*. Berkeley, Calif.: Tricycle Press, 1997.

Laird, Elizabeth. *Happy Birthday! A Book of Birthday Celebrations*. New York: Philomel, 1988.

Lorie, Peter. *Superstitions*. New York: Simon & Schuster, 1992.

Encarta 98 Encyclopedia. Microsoft, 1997.

Munan, Heidi. *Culture Shock! Malaysia*. Singapore: Times Books International, 1991.

Peng, Tan Huay. *Fun with Chinese Festivals*. Singapore: Federal Publications, 1991.

Perl, Lila. *Candles, Cakes, and Donkey Tails: Birthday Symbols and Celebrations*. New York: Clarion Books, 1984.

————. *Don't Sing Before Breakfast, Don't Sleep in the Moonlight: Everyday Superstitions and How They Began*. New York: Clarion Books, 1988.

Potter, Carole. *Knock on Wood: An Encyclopedia of Talismans, Charms, Superstitions and Symbols*. New York: Beaufort Books, 1983.

Rinkoff, Barbara. *Birthday Parties Around the World*. New York: M. Barrows, distributed by William Morrow, 1967.

Rotarian, October 1997.

Strong, James. *Strong's Exhaustive Concordance of the Bible*. Nashville, Tenn.: Thomas Nelson, n.d.

Waring, Philippa, ed. *The Dictionary of Omens & Superstitions*. Secaucus, N.J.: Chartwell Books, 1986.

1998 World Almanac and Book of Facts. Mahwah, N.J.: World Almanac Books, 1997.

INDEX